My Favorite Dogs

BULLDOG

Jinny Johnson

A+

Smart Apple Media

Published by Smart Apple Media
P.O. Box 1329
Mankato, MN 56002

Printed in the United States of America,
at Corporate Graphics in North Mankato, Minnesota.

Designed by Hel James
Edited by Mary-Jane Wilkins

Library of Congress Cataloging-in-Publication Data

Johnson, Jinny, 1949-
  Bulldog / by Jinny Johnson.
      p. cm. -- (My favorite dogs)
  Includes index.
  Summary: "Describes the care, training, and rearing of the bulldog. Also
explains the bulldog's unique characteristics and history"--Provided by
publisher.
  ISBN 978-1-59920-841-1 (hardcover : library bound)
  1. Bulldog--Juvenile literature. I. Title.
  SF429.B85J64 2013
  636.72--dc23
                        2012012142

Photo acknowledgements
t = top, b = bottom
page 1 WilleeCole/Shutterstock; 3 WilleeCole/Shutterstock; 4 godrick/
Shutterstock; 7 Brian Chase/Shutterstock; 8-9 iStockphoto/Thinkstock;
10 iStockphoto/Thinkstock; 11 Hemera/Thinkstock; 12t&b WilleeCole/
Shutterstock; 13 iStockphoto/Thinkstock; 14 WilleeCole/Shutterstock;
15 Patrick Johnson/Shutterstock; 16 Hemera/Thinkstock; 17 iStockphoto/
Thinkstock; 18-19 Hemera/Thinkstock; 20 WilleeCole/Shutterstock;
21 Katsai Tetiana/Shutterstock; 22 Sergey Goruppa/Shutterstock;
23 iStockphoto/Thinkstock
Cover iStockphoto/Thinkstock

DAD0504
042012
9 8 7 6 5 4 3 2 1

Contents

I'm a Bulldog!

Some people think I look fierce or sad, but I'm really very gentle and playful.

I'm a great family dog and I love being with people—especially children.

What I Need

I enjoy a walk every day, but I find it hard to walk fast for long. I don't like hot weather so I need shade on a sunny day. Never leave me outside in the heat.

I'm happy in the house, but I don't like to be left alone for long. I'm very cuddly and I like to snuggle up with my owners while they relax.

Be warned—I often snore loudly in my sleep and I sometimes drool!

7

The Bulldog

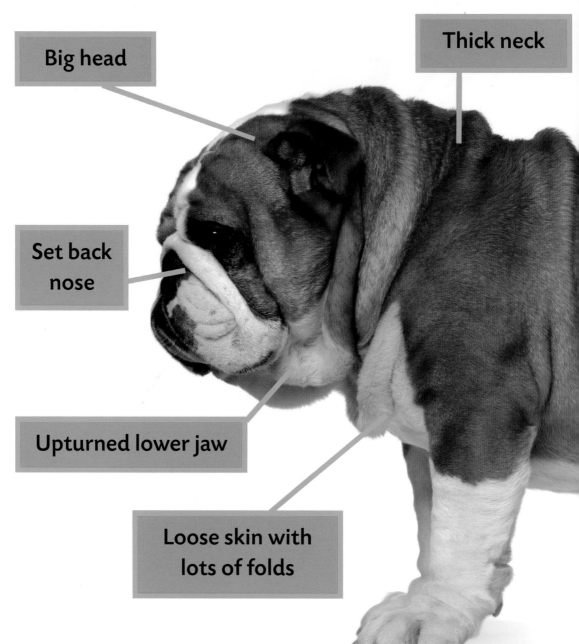

Big head

Thick neck

Set back nose

Upturned lower jaw

Loose skin with lots of folds

Weight: 40-50 pounds (18–23 kg)
Height: 12-14 inches (30–36 cm)

Color: brindle (brownish with streaks of other colors), red, fawn, or white, or a mix of white and color

Sturdy body

Short tail

Smooth coat

Short, thick legs

All About Bulldogs

Long ago, English bulldogs were bred as fighting dogs and they had to be strong and tough. Those fights don't happen now.

Today's bulldogs are not bred for fighting or sport. They are not fierce or aggressive, just good, loving pets.

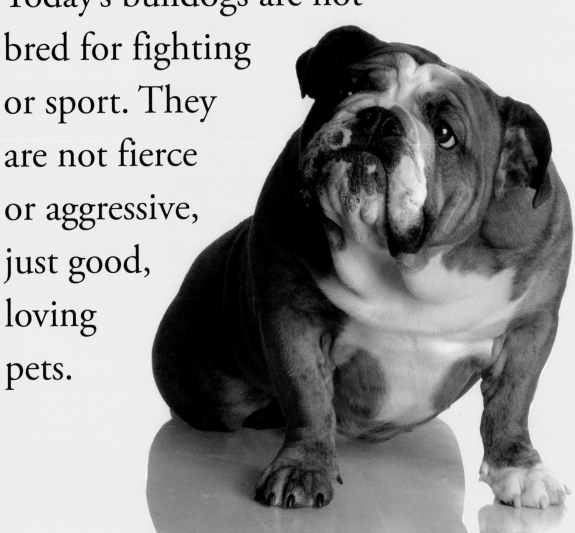

Bulldogs are popular mascots for college sports teams. Yale University's bulldog mascot is called Handsome Dan. A bulldog appears in *Lady and the Tramp* and other Disney cartoons, and in *Tom and Jerry*.

Growing Up

A bulldog puppy looks so cute with his big sad eyes and wrinkly face.

Like all pups, a bulldog misses his mom when he first goes to his new home. Be extra kind and gentle with your new pup and he will soon learn to love his human family.

Training Your Bulldog

A well-trained bulldog that knows his place in the family is a happy bulldog. Bulldogs aren't difficult to train, but they are stubborn and they are not good at paying attention for long.

It's best to keep training times short and to repeat them often.

Reward your bulldog when he does well and never shout at him.

15

French Bulldog

This little dog is about half the weight of an English bulldog. He doesn't mind being inside a lot, so he makes a good pet if you live in an apartment. He is very loving and good natured.

The French bulldog loves to sit on his owner's lap and be pet and cuddled.

American Bulldog

The American bulldog has longer legs and a slimmer body than the English bulldog. He runs fast and is more active, so needs more exercise.

These dogs were bred as working dogs for farmers and ranchers. They are larger and heavier than English bulldogs.

Your Healthy Bulldog

A bulldog's short hair only needs brushing once a week to keep his coat healthy. Give him a bath if he gets very dirty and muddy.

Dirt can get trapped in a bulldog's skin folds. Check the folds

regularly and clean them with
a tissue when necessary.

Take extra care of your bulldog
in the summer. He may have
difficulty breathing in hot weather.

Caring For Your Bulldog

You and your family must think very carefully before buying a bulldog. He will live for at least eight years and need lots of attention.

Be careful not to overfeed your bulldog,

as he doesn't exercise as much as some dogs. He should go out every day—even if he seems to prefer lying on the sofa.

He will also need to go to the vet for regular checks and vaccinations.

Useful Words

aggressive
An aggressive animal is likely to get into fights and attack others.

mascot
Something that people believe brings them good luck.

vaccination
An injection that can help protect your dog from illness.

Index